JEWISH COOKING

Designed by Claire Leighton
Food photography by Peter Barry
Recipes prepared and styled by Helen Burdett
Edited by Jillian Stewart

CLB 2627
© 1991 Colour Library Books Ltd., Godalming, Surrey, England
All rights reserved
This 1993 edition published by Crescent Books,
distributed by Outlet Book Company, Inc., a Random House Company
40 Engelhard Avenue, Avenel, New Jersey 07001
Printed and bound in Singapore
ISBN 0 517 06146 5
7 6 5 4 3 2 1

JEWISH COOKING

CRESCENT BOOKS
NEW YORK · AVENEL, NEW JERSEY

INTRODUCTION

Legend has it that the art of Jewish cooking was born on the day recorded in Genesis when the matriarch Rebecca, by skillful use of herbs and spices, persuaded her husband Isaac that the casserole she had made using the insipid meat from a young kid was really succulent wild venison. Rebecca's culinary philosophy of "taste with economy" has been followed by Jewish cooks ever since.

Jewish dietary laws have many prohibitions: no shellfish, no pig, no carrion, no birds of prey, nothing that crawls upon its belly. Then there are strict categories of food that are permitted: only those fish that have fins and scales; only those animals that chew the cud and have cloven hooves. There are also many cooking and serving instructions. Meat and poultry must be soaked and salted to purge it of blood before it is cooked. Foods of dairy and animal origin cannot be combined either in the cooking or the serving of a meal, and dairy foods can be eaten after a meat meal only after several hours have elapsed.

However, it was in the Ten Commandments that there appeared those instructions which have resulted in the development of some of the most typical of Jewish foods – dishes that can be cooked one day and served on the next. For the Fourth Commandment forbids work of any kind on the Sabbath. It became customary to spend Thursday and most of Friday before dusk in the kitchen, preparing dishes for Sabbath lunch.

Jewish cooking has had other influences. As the Jewish people spread throughout the world, often forced to move from country to country in order to avoid persecution, they adopted and adapted many of the recipes and ingredients they found in their new homelands. In Eastern Europe, for example, kosher meat was frequently in short supply, and so the little that was available had to be "stretched" by using it as a stuffing for a variety of doughs and vegetables, such as "Holishkes" (stuffed cabbage leaves), or "Kreplach" (ground meat stuffing in a noodle dough). Today, Jewish cooking reflects a multitude of ethnic influences from as far afield as Spain, Germany, Poland, Russia and the Middle East.

Today almost every "traditional" Jewish dish can be bought ready to eat, whether it be chicken soup and kreplach in a can, gefilte fish in a jar, even Sabbath chicken in a frozen pack. But nothing can ever replace the glorious flavors and perfumes of home-cooked Jewish food.

Right: a bustling Sunday street market on New York's Lower East Side— traditionally a Jewish neighborhood.

Chicken Soup with Kreplach

Ingredients
Whole or half fowl with the feet, wings and giblets
7½ cups water
1 whole onion, peeled
2 carrots, peeled and cut into 4
Leaves and top 2 inches of
    2 stalks celery
1 sprig of parsley

1 very ripe tomato
2 tsps salt
Pinch of white pepper
Any soft eggs from the fowl
Sprigs of chervil to garnish

Dough
2 cups all-purpose flour
2 eggs

Pinch of salt
1 tbsp plus 2 tsps lukewarm water

Filling
½ a medium onion, peeled and
    cut in 1 inch chunks
1lb shin beef, cooked and
    cut in 1 inch cubes

1 egg
½ level tsp salt
Speck of white pepper

Put the water, salt and pepper into a large, heavy soup pan, and add the feet, wings, giblets and the bird. Cover and bring to the boil. Uncover and remove any froth. Add all the remaining main ingredients. Bring back to the boil, then reduce the heat, cover and continue to simmer for a further 3 hours.

Strain the soup into one bowl and put the giblets and the carrots into another. The fowl should be put in a separate container for further use. Next day, remove any congealed fat and return the soup to the pan. Add the cooked giblets and the carrot (cut into small dice).

Make the dough with the metal blade of the food processor, process the flour, eggs and salt until thoroughly blended, slowly add the water. Process for a further 40 seconds, then turn it out on to a floured board. Knead briefly with the heel of the hand then cover with a large bowl and leave to "relax" for 20 minutes.

To make the kreplach filling, pulse the onion and meat in the food processor just until finely ground. Add the egg and seasonings and process until evenly moistened. Turn into a bowl.

To shape the dough, divide the dough in two, roll each piece on a floured board until paper-thin. Roll each sheet into a flattened jelly roll about 3 inches in diameter and cut it into slices each 2 inches wide. Have ready a 10 cups pan half-full of boiling water with 2 teaspoons of salt in it. Unroll the strips of dough and pile these strips on top of each other. Cut them in 2 inch squares. Put a teaspoon of the meat filling in the center of each square then fold over into a triangle, pressing the edges securely to seal dampen them with water only if necessary. As each one is finished lay it on a sheet of wax paper.

Add one-half of the kreplach to the boiling water, bring back to the boil, cover and cook for 15 minutes, tasting after 10 minutes to see if they are tender. Drain and reserve. Repeat with the remaining kreplach.

To serve, add kreplach to the soup, reheat slowly 5 to 10 minutes before serving.

Borscht

Serves: 6-8   **Freeze:** 3 months   **Keeps:** 2 days under refrigeration

Ingredients

2lbs old beets or
    3 bunches of young beets
1 medium carrot, peeled
1 medium onion, peeled
6 cups water or meat or
  chicken stock

15 grinds of black pepper
2 tsps salt (if water is used)
2 tbsps sugar

To thicken

3 tbsps lemon juice

3 whole eggs

Have ready a 10-cup soup pan. Trim the beets then peel or scrape. Cut all the vegetables into 1-inch chunks, then process in the food processor in two batches until very finely chopped. Put in the pan with the water or stock, pepper, salt (if used) and sugar. Bring to the boil, cover and simmer for 20 minutes until the vegetables are soft and the liquid is a rich dark red.

Pour the contents through a coarse strainer into a bowl and discard the vegetables, then return the strained beet juice to the pan and leave on a low heat. Put the lemon juice and the whole eggs into the food processor and process for 5 seconds until well mixed. With the motor running, pour two ladles of the hot beet juice through the feed tube and process for a further 3 seconds, then add to the beet juice in the pan and heat gently, whisking constantly with a batter whisk until the soup is steaming and has thickened slightly. Do not let it boil or it will curdle. Taste and adjust the seasoning so that there is a gentle blend of sweet and sour. The soup reheats well.

The Western Wall of Solomon's Temple in Jerusalem is Judaism's holiest shrine.

Chopped Liver

Freeze: 3 months   **Keeps:** 3 days under refrigeration

Ingredients

3 hard-cooked eggs, plus
   1 extra egg for garnish
1 large onion, finely chopped
1 medium clove of garlic, crushed
1/4 cup soft margarine or 3 rounded
   tbsps rendered chicken fat

1 tsp sea salt
20 grinds black pepper
Good pinch ground nutmeg
1lb chicken livers (quartered)
Watercress sprigs for garnish

Hard-cook the eggs for 10 minutes then leave in the pan covered with cold water. Fry the onion and the garlic gently in the fat until a rich brown (this is important if the right depth of flavor is to be achieved). As the onion cooks, sprinkle it with the sea salt and pepper. Lift out onto a plate. Add the livers to the fat and stir well, cooking gently for 5 minutes.

Shell and halve the 3 eggs.

Put the onion and the garlic with their juices into the food processor and process until smooth, then add the remaining ingredients and process again until smooth. Taste, and add more seasoning if necessary, but remember the flavor will intensify over the next few hours. Turn into a terrine or oval gratin dish, or divide between individual cocottes. Chill, covered with saranwrap, preferably overnight. Refrigerate the extra egg.

One hour before serving, remove the pâté from the refrigerator and leave at room temperature.

Just before serving, grate the remaining egg and use it to decorate the top of the pâté along with the watercress. Serve with warm French bread or slices of chalah (Jewish plaited bread).

The ancient ruins of the Jewish hilltop fortress of Masada are evocative of its turbulent past.

Pickled Herring

Serves: 4 people on 3 occasions   **Keeps:** 1 month under refrigeration

Ingredients

6 milt (soft roe) herring
White pepper
2 medium onions, thinly sliced
1 large unpeeled lemon, sliced

2 bay leaves and a dried chili pepper
1 tbsp pickling spice
2½ cups white vinegar
2 tbsps brown sugar

Behead the herring, slit open and remove the entrails. Put the fish in a glass casserole (so that the smell will not linger) and put under the cold water tap. Leave the water running in a gentle trickle. After an hour, turn off the tap and leave the herring overnight covered in cold water. Next day, lift them out of the water and drain well. Put on paper towels and scrape with a blunt knife to remove loose scales. Wash again under the cold water tap and put on a board. Open the front, then turn over and press the back with the flat of the hand. Turn over again and you will find that the backbone can be lifted out easily. Remove any other loose bones. Sprinkle each herring very lightly with white pepper, add two or three thin rings of onion, then roll up from tail to head. If the herring are very large, you may find it easier to split them lengthwise before rolling. Skewer each herring closed with a wooden pick. Put in a glass jar in alternate layers with the sliced lemon, the remaining onion, the bay leaves and the spices.

Put the vinegar and sugar into a pan and bring to the boil. Immediately the liquid bubbles, turn off the heat and leave until it is lukewarm. Pour over the herring. Cover and refrigerate for 4 days before using. Serve in ½-inch slices, either speared on wooden picks or as an hors d'oeuvre garnished with the pickled onion slices, tomato and cucumber.

An almost timeless scene as fishermen land the day's catch from the
Sea of Galilee.

Knishes
(Potato-Filled Pastries)

Makes: 24 **Freeze:** 3 months, raw or cooked **Keeps:** 2 days under refrigeration

Ingredients
Pastry

2 cups all-purpose flour mixed
   with a pinch of salt
1 tsp confectioners' sugar
²/₃ cup firm butter or block
   margarine cut in 1-inch cubes

1 egg
1 tsp wine vinegar
1 tbsp icy water
Further 2 tbsps firm
   butter or margarine

Filling

1 cup chopped onions
6 tbsps butter or margarine
2 cups mashed potato
1 egg
¼ tsp pepper

Sesame or poppy seeds
Beaten egg to glaze

To make the pastry, sift the dry ingredients into a bowl and add the ²/₃ cup of fat, then rub it in until no pieces larger than a small pea come to the surface when the bowl is shaken. Whisk the the egg, vinegar and water to blend, sprinkle over the mixture in the bowl, then mix to a dough.

On a floured board, roll the dough mixed by either method into a rectangle about 12 x 6 inches and spread the top two thirds with little dabs of the extra 2 tablespoons of fat. Fold in three, as for flaky pastry, seal the ends and sides with the rolling pin, then gently flatten and roll out again. Fold in three once more, seal as before, then chill for at least 1 hour or overnight. (The dough may also be frozen at this stage.)

To make the filling, heat the butter or margarine and sauté the onion until golden. Combine with all the other ingredients, except seeds, in a bowl and stir well to blend.

To shape and fill the knishes, preheat the oven to 425°F. Have ready two ungreased cookie sheets. Roll out the chilled pastry ¼-inch thick and cut into 3-inch rounds with a plain cutter. Put a rounded teaspoon of the filling in the center of each round, then fold into a half-moon and seal the edges. Arrange on the sheets and brush with the beaten egg, then scatter with the sesame or poppy seeds. Bake for 15-20 minutes or until a rich brown. Cool for 15 minutes before serving, or reheat later.

Herring and Apple Salad in Sour Cream Sauce

Serves: 6-8   **Keeps:** 2 days under refrigeration

Ingredients
1 jar (16oz) pickled herring
1 medium mild onion, white or red
  salad variety if possible

4 crisp tart dessert apples
  (about 1lb in weight)

Sauce
1¼ cups sour cream
1 tsp wine vinegar

½ tsp superfine sugar
½ tsp Dijon or other mild mustard

Garnish
Shredded lettuce

Paprika

Drain the herring thoroughly on paper towels, discarding the pickled onions and liquid from the jar. Slice the onion finely, then cut each slice into two or three sections. Core and peel the apples, cut each into eight and then cut each section across into ½-inch slices. Cut the herring into slanting slices of a similar size. Put the herring, onion and apple into a large bowl. Stir the vinegar and seasonings into the soured cream then stir it gently through the apple and herring mixture. Refrigerate for several hours or overnight.

Spoon the salad on to a bed of shredded lettuce arranged on individual plates, and garnish with a pinch of paprika. Serve with buttered rye or wholewheat bread.

Charoseth
(Passover Nut and Apple Pâté)

Keeps: 2 days under refrigeration

Ingredients
¾ cup walnuts
¼ large cooking apple
Kosher wine to moisten

2 tsps cinnamon
2 tsps sugar

Mince or process the walnuts and the apple until puréed. Moisten with the kosher wine and flavor with the cinnamon and sugar. The consistency should be that of mortar.

Gefilte Fish (Poached)

Makes: 12-14 fish balls **Serves:** 6-7 **Freeze:** 3 months **Keeps:** 3 days in refrigerator

Ingredients

1lb haddock fillet, skinned –
   or other firm-fleshed white
1lb cod fillet, skinned
1 medium onion, peeled
2 eggs

2 tsp salt
Pinch of white pepper
2 tsps sugar
1 tbsp sunflower oil
½ cup medium matzah meal

Stock

1 cleaned fish head
Skin and bones from the fish
2 tsps salt
Water to cover the bones

1 medium onion, thinly sliced
2 medium carrots, sliced ¼-inch thick
2 tsps sugar

Wash and salt the fish and leave to drain. Cut the onion in 1-inch chunks and put into the food processor with the eggs, seasonings and oil, then process until reduced to a smooth purée. Pour this purée into a large bowl and stir in the matzah meal. Leave to swell for 10 minutes.

Cut the fish into 1-inch chunks and put in the processor, half-filling the bowl each time. Process for 5 seconds, until the fish is finely chopped then add to the egg and onion purée and blend in using a large fork. Repeat until all the fish has been processed, then mix thoroughly. The mixture should be firm enough to shape into a soft ball. If it feels to "cloggy", rinse out the processor bowl with a tablespoon or two of water and stir that in. If it feels very soft, stir in a tablespoon or two of matzah meal. Leave for half an hour, or overnight (under refrigeration) if preferred.

To shape into balls, dip the hands into cold water and form the mixture into balls about the size of a small apple.

To poach the gefilte fish, first simmer the head, skin and bones of the fish with the salt and cold water to cover for 30 minutes, then remove the skin and bones (leave in the head as this helps the stock to gel). Add the onion, carrots, sugar and balls of fish. Bring to the boil, then turn the heat low, cover the pan and simmer for 1½ hours, uncover and simmer for a further 30 minutes to concentrate the stock. Lift out the balls and arrange them on a platter, topping each fish ball with a slice of carrot. Pour the stock through a strainer over the fish, then chill overnight before serving.

Fried Fish

Serves: 6-8   **Freeze:** 3 months   **Keeps:** 3 days under refrigeration

Ingredients

6-8 fillets or steaks of any white fish (steaks should be cut ¾-1-inch thick, fillets should be 1-inch thick)
1 egg

1 cup (approx) dry coating crumbs or matzah meal
2 tbsps all-purpose flour
Sunflower or other flavorless vegetable oil for frying

Garnish

Lemon slices

Fresh dill

Wash the fish under cold running water, arrange round the sides of a colander, sprinkle lightly with kosher salt and leave to drain. Beat the egg with a fork to blend then put into a shallow dish. Put the coating crumbs in another dish and the flour in a third dish. Dip each piece of fish in and out of the flour, patting off any surplus, then dip it in and out of the egg and finally lay it in the crumbs and pat them on in an even layer.

Remove the frying basket from a deep fat fryer and heat the oil to 375°. Lower 3-4 pieces of fish into the deep fryer. Do not crowd the pan. Cover and cook 7 minutes for fillets, 8 minutes for steaks. Drain on crumpled paper towels. Serve garnished with lemon slices and dill.

The Judean wilderness has changed little over the centuries.

Chicken Paprikash

Serves: 6-8   **Keeps:** 3 days under refrigeration   **Freeze:** 2 months

Ingredients

2 x 3½lb chickens, backbone
   removed and each cut in 4
       OR
8 chicken portions on the bone

3 tbsps sunflower oil
2 medium onions, finely chopped
4 tbsps Hungarian paprika
1¼ cups chicken stock

4 medium green or red pepper
   cut into ½ inch strips
1 x 14 oz can chopped tomatoes
2 tsps brown sugar
2 tsps cornstarch slaked with
   2 tbsps cold water
1 tsp salt
10 grinds black pepper

Dry the chicken pieces with paper towels then sauté in the hot oil until golden. Remove. In the remaining oil, gently cook the onion (covered) for 10-15 minutes until softened and golden. Stir in the paprika and 10 fl oz chicken stock and cook for a further 2 minutes. Add the chicken and any juices, the pepper strips, the tomatoes and the sugar and sprinkle with the salt and pepper. Cover and cook very gently for 25-30 minutes until the chicken is cooked through – there will be no sign of pinkness when a piece is nicked with a sharp knife. Lift the chicken pieces onto a warm platter. Add the cornstarch mixed with the water, and add to the pan. Simmer for 3 minutes or until thickened to a coating consistency, add the salt and pepper, taste and adjust the seasoning if necessary. Spoon the sauce over the chicken and serve.

Israel's fertile farmland provides produce for the main towns and cities.

Braised Brisket with Carrots

Serves: 4-6   **Freeze:** 3 months   **Keeps:** 3 days under refrigeration

Ingredients

3lbs brisket
1 tbsp meat fat
6 peppercorns
2 tsps salt
10 grinds black pepper

1 bay leaf
6 pickling (small) onions
$\frac{1}{3}$ cup boiling water
2 large potatoes
2 medium carrots

Brown the meat quickly in the hot fat. Sprinkle with the seasonings and bay leaf. Put in a casserole surrounded with the onions and the boiling water. Cover and cook in a slow oven, 300°F, for 3 hours. One hour before the meat is ready, surround it with thick slices of potato and carrot.

Serve the brisket cut in thick slices together with the potatoes and carrots in the delicious meat juices.

A Kiddush cup, which is used before the meal on the eve of the Sabbath.

Chuck Pot Roast

Serves: 6-8   **Freeze:** 3 months

Ingredients

2 tbsps oil
3-4lbs chuck beef with
    1 tsp salt, 1 tsp
    dry mustard and 2 tsps
    flour rubbed into the raw surface
2 small onions, coarsely sliced
Salt
Black pepper

2 stalks celery, coarsely sliced
2 carrots, coarsely sliced
½ green pepper, coarsely sliced
1 bay leaf
A sprig of parsley
1 clove garlic
⅓ cup water

Set the oven to 325°F. In a heavy-based casserole, heat the oil and brown the floured meat quickly on all sides. Lift it out onto a plate. Into the same oil, put the sliced onions, cooking them until soft and golden (this is important as it helps to color the sauce). Add all the remaining vegetables and stir them well to absorb any remaining oil. Sprinkle with a little additional salt and 10 grinds of black pepper. Add the bay leaf, parsley, garlic and water. Stir the contents of the casserole thoroughly, then replace the browned meat on the vegetable bed. Cover and put in the oven. When the liquid starts to bubble (after about 15 minutes) turn the oven down to 300°F and cook for 2½-3 hours. Allow 40 minutes per pound plus 40 minutes extra. Ten minutes before serving, take off the lid and allow the surface of the meat to dry off.

Put the meat on a hot dish, push all the vegetables and juices through a sieve into a small pan or process until smooth. Skim off any excess fat, heat to boiling, season with salt and pepper and serve with the meat cut into thin slices. Serve with boiled potatoes and a green vegetable.

Meat Loaf

Serves: 6 with leftovers **Freeze:** 2 months **Keeps:** 2 days under refrigeration

Ingredients

2lbs ground beef
3 large slices bread
2 eggs
1 medium onion
1 tsp dry mustard

1 tbsp tomato catsup
1 tbsp dark soy sauce
2 tsp salt
Pinch of black pepper
1 tbsp medium matzah meal

Gravy

1 small onion, finely chopped
1 tbsp margarine

1 cup beef stock
2 tsps cornstarch

Into the food processor put the bread, eggs, onion cut in four, mustard, sauces and seasonings. Process for one minute or until smooth. Mix thoroughly with meat and matzah meal in a large bowl. Pack into a loaf tin about 9 x 5 x 3 inches, pressing down well, then turn out into a roasting tin just big enough to leave a 1-inch margin all the way round. Put in a quick oven 400°F for 15 minutes then turn oven down to 350°F for a further 45 minutes.

Whilst meat is cooking, fry the onion in the margarine until golden brown then stir in the beef stock mixed with the cornstarch. Bring to the boil then pour over and round the meat loaf 15 minutes before the end of cooking.

Serve the meat loaf with gravy in slices. If meat loaf is to be served cold, there is no need for gravy.

Potato Latkes

Serves: 4

Ingredients

4 medium-sized potatoes, peeled
1 onion
2 tbsps flour

1 egg, beaten
Salt and pepper
Oil for frying

Soak the potatoes in cold water for 30 minutes. Pat them dry, and then grate finely. Peel and grate the onion finely, and combine with the potato. Place the mixture in a colander and press to drain off the excess moisture. Combine the potato mixture with the flour and the egg. Season to taste.

Heat ¼ inch of oil in a frying pan. Drop tablespoonfuls of the latke mixture into the pan, and fry for about 2 minutes, until the underside browns. Turn and brown on the other side. Drain and serve immediately, either on their own or with sour cream.

Cholent
(Sabbath Lima Bean Casserole)

Serves: 6   **Freeze:** 1 month   **Keeps:** 3 days under refrigeration

Ingredients

2½ cups dried lima beans
3lb piece of boneless brisket
Salt
Pepper
Paprika
Ginger
¼ cup margarine

3 sliced onions
1 clove garlic, crushed
1 bay leaf
6 peeled whole potatoes or
   1⅓ cups barley
Freshly chopped parsley

Cover the lima beans in cold water, soak overnight then drain well. Rub the brisket with the salt, pepper, paprika and ginger, then brown quickly in the margarine, together with the onions and the garlic. Put in a deep earthenware casserole (a Dutch oven is ideal). Add the bay leaf, drained soaked beans, and the potatoes or barley. Barely cover with boiling water, cover the dish and put in a quick oven, 400°F, for 30 minutes or until the contents start to bubble. Turn the heat down to 250°F and leave overnight. Serve for lunch the next day sprinkled with freshly chopped parsley.

The Star of David under the Damascus Gate in Jerusalem.

Stuffed Peppers

Serves: 4-6   **Freeze:** 2 months   **Keeps:** 3 days under refrigeration

Ingredients

4-6 medium green or red peppers
1lb lean ground beef
1 onion, grated
1 egg

1 tsp salt
½ tsp mustard
Pinch of pepper

Sauce

1 medium onion
2 tbsps oil
5oz can tomato paste and
   2 cans water
4 tbsps brown sugar

2 tbsps lemon juice
½ tsp mixed spice
⅔ cup white wine
   (optional but nice)

If the peppers are to be stewed on top of the stove, use the same pan to make the sauce. Chop the onion finely, then sauté in the oil until soft and golden. Add all the remaining sauce ingredients and simmer uncovered for 20 minutes.

Slice the tops off the peppers and remove the seeds and ribs. Put into a pan with the lids and pour over boiling water. Leave for 5 minutes. Beat the egg, grate the onion, add the salt mustard and pepper, then mix in the meat. Drain the peppers, stuff with the meat mixture and replace lids. Put into the pan where the sauce is simmering. Cover with foil and then with the lid of the pan. Simmer gently for one hour, basting twice. When done, the sauce will be thick and the peppers tender.

To cook in the oven, simmer at 325°F for 1½ hours.

A Jewish vendor sells freshly baked bagels on the streets of New York.

Stuffed Cabbage Rolls in a Sweet-Sour Tomato Sauce

Serves: 6 as a starter, 4 as a main course   **Freeze:** 3 months
Keeps: 3 day under refrigeration

Ingredients

1 firm head white cabbage
1 onion, finely chopped
2 tbsps chicken fat or
    2oz margarine
3-4 tbsps Basmati
    (long grain) rice

½ cup chicken stock
1lb ground beef
Salt
Pepper

The sauce

5oz tomato paste
1¼ cups water
½ tsp salt

10 grinds black pepper
4 tbsps brown sugar
Juice of a large lemon

To separate the cabbage leaves, freeze the whole cabbage for 3 days then leave to thaw overnight at room temperature. Use a knife to detach at least 12 leaves from the tough stalk.

To make the filling, cook the onion in the chicken fat or margarine till tender and golden then add the rice and cook a further 3 minutes until opaque. Add the stock and cook till absorbed then stir into the meat with the seasonings. One by one put the cabbage leaves on the table, put on a tablespoon of the filling, fold and roll like parcels, then squeeze gently between the palms to seal. Place in a casserole.

Make the sauce by mixing all the sauce ingredients thoroughly. Cover the rolls with the sauce and cook 300°F, covered, for 2 hours. Uncover, and turn up to 350°F for a further half hour to brown the rolls and thicken the sauce.

Cows grazing in Galilee. Much Jewish cooking involves the use of dairy produce.

Tsimmes with Dumpling
(Carrot and Beef Casserole)

Serves: 6　**Keeps:** 3 days under refrigeration

Ingredients
2lb slice of brisket　　　　Pepper
3lbs carrots　　　　　　　1 tbsp cornstarch
4 tbsps corn syrup　　　　1½lbs potatoes
2 tsps salt

Dumpling
⅓ cup margarine　　　　　½ tsp salt
1½ cups all-purpose flour　3-4 tbsps water to mix
1½ tsps baking powder

Trim excess fat off the meat, leaving a thin edging, then cut into 1½-inch chunks. Peel the carrots and cut into ½-inch cubes. Put the carrots and meat into a pan, barely cover with hot water, and add 2 tablespoons of the syrup, pepper to taste and ½ teaspoon of salt, bring to the boil and simmer for 2 hours, either on top of the stove, or in a slow oven. Skim, or if possible chill, so that most of the fat can be removed.

Four hours before you want the tsimmes, make the dumpling by rubbing the margarine into the dry ingredients. Mix to a soft dough with the water. Put the dumpling in the middle of a large oval earthenware, enamel or enamelled iron casserole. Arrange the drained meat and carrots around it. Mix the cornstarch with enough water to make a smooth cream, then stir into the stock from the carrots and meat. Bring to the boil then pour over the carrots and meat. Peel and cut the potatoes into large cubes and arrange on top, adding extra boiling water if necessary so that they are just submerged. Sprinkle with the remaining teaspoon of salt and 2 tablespoons of corn syrup. Cover and bring to the boil on top of the stove then transfer to a slow oven, 300°F, for 3½ hours. Uncover and taste, adding a little more syrup if necessary. Allow to brown, uncovered, for a further half an hour, then serve. The potatoes and the dumpling should be slightly brown and the sauce slightly thickened.

Kasha Varnishkes
(Buckwheat with Pasta)

Serves: 6   **Freeze:** 3 months   **Keeps:** 3 days under refrigeration

Ingredients
2 cups roasted buckwheat
1 egg, beaten
2 cups boiling water
1 tsp paprika
1 tsp salt
10 grinds black pepper

1 large onion
3 tbsps margarine or
    chicken fat
3-4 tbsps leftover beef of
    chicken gravy (optional)
1 cup cooked pasta bows

Put the buckwheat into a large sauté pan and add the beaten egg, mix well and cook over medium heat for 5 minutes, stirring occasionally until the groats look puffy and dry. Add the boiling water and the seasonings, cover and simmer for 15 minutes until the liquid is absorbed. Meanwhile, gently sauté the finely-chopped onion in the fat in a covered pan until soft and golden, then add to the cooked buckwheat, stirring well. Stir in the cooked pasta and the gravy if used and reheat until steaming. May be left to cool and reheated when required.

A Hasidic Jew prays at the Wailing Wall.

Cheese Blintzes

Makes: 12   **Freeze:** unfilled pancakes 3 months, filled blintzes 1 month

Ingredients
Batter

1 cup all-purpose flour
Pinch of salt
2 large eggs
½ cup milk

½ cup water
2 tsps flavorless oil
Butter and oil for frying

Filling

1½ cups dry cottage cheese or other soft white cheese mixed with 2 tbsps
    light cream or an egg yolk
1 tsp sugar
Pinch of salt

Sift the flour and salt into a bowl. Make a well, drop in eggs and flavorless oil and start stirring in the surrounding flour to make a stirrable batter. Gradually add the milk and water until smooth. Beat with a whisk until the surface is covered with tiny bubbles. Leave the batter for half an hour. If you have a blender or food processor, put liquids into the bowl followed by the dry ingredients and blend until a smooth batter is formed. Blend all the filling ingredients together and leave until required.

To fry the pancakes, stir the batter well and pour into a jug. It should be the consistency of light cream. If too thick, add a further tablespoonsful of water. Use a 6-inch diameter omelet or crèpe pan with rounded sides. Put on medium heat for 3 minutes then drop in a teaspoon of oil and swirl it round the base and sides of the pan. Wipe out any excess oil with paper towels, then again using paper towels, smear the entire inner surface of the pan very thinly with butter, then pour in a thick layer of batter, swirling it round so that it covers the sides as well as the base of the pan. The heat will immediately set a thin layer so that the excess can be poured back into the jug. By this means you will get a blintze so thin that by the time the sides of the pancake begin to curl from the pan, the bottom will be brown and the top side dry. Turn the pancake out onto a sheet of wax paper covering a wooden board. Re-butter the pan and repeat the process until all the batter has been used. As each pancake stops steaming, stack one on top of the other, browned side up. At this stage pancakes can be frozen, refrigerated overnight, or stuffed.

To stuff the pancakes, place a pancake brown side up on a board or counter. Spread a tablespoon of the filling thinly over the bottom half, turn in the sides and roll up into a long thin roll. Repeat with each pancake.

To serve – heat ¼ cup butter and 2 teaspoons of oil in a wide frying pan. The moment the butter stops foaming, put in the blintzes, join side upwards. Cook gently for 3 minutes until golden brown, turn and cook the second side.

Apricot Eingemachtes
(Passover Apricot Jam)

Makes: 4 pounds   **Keeps:** 12 months in a cool, ventilated cupboard

Ingredients
3 cups dried apricots
5 cups cold water
4 cups granulated sugar

4 tbsps fresh lemon juice
¾ cup almonds, blanched and split

The night before you plan to make the eingemachtes, put the fruit in a preserving pan or other heavy pan of 10 cup capacity and cover with water. The next day add more water if necessary to ensure the fruit is barely covered, half-cover the pan then bring to the boil and simmer until the apricots are absolutely tender (about 10 to 20 minutes). Meanwhile wash and rinse sufficient jars and put in a low oven, 225°F, to dry and warm.

Add the sugar to the tender fruit, stir until it has been dissolved, then add the lemon juice and the almonds and boil hard until the liquid has become a thick and viscous syrup. (Do not over boil or the sugar will begin to caramelize and spoil the delicate flavour of the eingemachtes.) Put into the warm dry jars and cover at once with wax discs. Leave to cool, then cover each jar with a lid which has a rubber seal.

The cultivation of citrus fruit plays a crucial part in the Israeli economy.

Hamantaschen
(Purim Pastries)

Makes: about 24   **Freeze:** 3 months   **Keeps:** 1 week in an airtight container

Ingredients
Filling
1 cup black poppyseeds
½ cup milk
2 tbsps butter
¼ cup superfine sugar
2 level tbsps corn syrup

½ cup walnuts, chopped
⅓ cup seedless raisins, chopped
½ tsp vanilla extract or
   grated lemon rind

The pastry
2 eggs (reserve a little for glazing)
⅔ cup superfine sugar
½ cup flavorless oil
1 tsp vanilla extract

Grated rind of ½ orange
3 cups all-purpose flour
1½ tsps baking powder

Put the poppyseeds through a foodmill or grind in a liquidizer, then stir in the milk followed by all the other ingredients except the vanilla extract or lemon rind. Cook in a small pan until thick (about 5 minutes). Taste and add more sugar as necessary. Add vanilla or lemon rind when cool.

Whisk the eggs until thick, then whisk in the sugar, oil and seasonings. Finally stir in enough flour to make a rollable dough. Roll out on a floured board until ¼-inch thick and cut into 3-inch rounds.

Place a spoonful of the cooled filling in the center of each round then draw up three sides to form a triangle and pinch the edges firmly together. Brush the tops with a little beaten egg. Bake in a moderate oven, 350°F, for 30 minutes. Cool on a cooling rack.

Kosher food is in plentiful supply in New York's Jewish neighborhoods.

Passover Spongecake

Makes: 1 9-inch cake **Freeze:** 3 months **Keeps:** 1 week in an airtight container

Ingredients
5 large eggs
1¼ cups superfine sugar
2 tsps lemon juice

⅔ cup cake meal
½ cup potato starch
Confectioners' sugar

Separate the egg yolks from the whites. Divide the sugar into two equal quantities. Put one amount of sugar into a bowl with the yolks and whisk until thick and white. (If an electric beater is not available, stand the eggs and sugar in a bowl over a pan of very hot water and whisk until thick and white.) Whisk in the lemon juice. In another bowl, whisk the whites until they form stiff, glossy peaks then whisk in the sugar a tablespoon at a time until a firm meringue is formed. Fold into the first mixture. Finally fold in the sifted meal and potato starch. Spoon into a 9 x 3-inch round cake pan which has been oiled and then sprinkled with sugar. Level the surface. Sprinkle a thin layer of superfine sugar over the top. Bake at 350°F for 1 hour 10 minutes.

All generations of a Jewish family gather for the traditional Passover meal.

Mohn Strudel
(Hungarian Poppyseed Yeast Dough Strudel)

Makes: 6 strudels   **Freeze:** 3 months   **Keeps:** 4 days under refrigeration

Ingredients

2 cups lukewarm milk
4 cakes fresh yeast
1 egg yolk
¾ cup soft butter

½ cup superfine sugar
6 cups all-purpose flour
2 tsps salt

Filling

2 cups ground or
　whole poppy seeds
1 cup milk
3 tbsps melted butter
Tart jam such as damson or 'povidl' (continental plum preserve)
Sifted confectioners' sugar

½ cup superfine sugar (or to taste)
Rind of 1 lemon, finely grated
1 cup white raisins

The dough is best made with an electric mixer or wooden spoon, as it is rather too soft to use a dough hook. Put the warm milk and the fresh yeast in the mixing bowl and stir until the yeast has dissolved. Add all the remaining dough ingredients. Now beat until the dough is smooth and stretchy and can be pulled away from the beaters leaving them almost clean. This will take about 5 minutes. Tip the dough out of the bowl, grease the bowl with oil, then put the dough back in and turn it to cover it lightly with oil. Cover with saranwrap and leave in a warm kitchen until it has doubled in volume, about 1½ hours.

If the poppyseeds are whole, grind them in a nut or coffee mill until they are like ground almonds, then put them in a pan with the rest of the filling ingredients, except the jam and confectioners sugar. Bring to the boil, stirring, then bubble for 5 minutes until the filling is thick but juicy. Allow to go cold.

To assemble the strudel, tip the risen dough on to a floured board and knead with the hands for 2 minutes, then divide into six equal pieces (weighing approximately 8 ounces each). Knead each piece into a ball. Roll each ball into a rectangle ⅛ -inch thick and measuring 11 x 6 inches. Spread first with a thin layer of melted butter and then with some jam, then spread thickly all over with the filling. Turn in the short ends and roll up into a strudel. Put the strudels on greased sheets, join side down, leaving room for each strudel to almost double in size. Put each tray in a large plastic bag and leave for 30 minutes or until the strudels are puffy and will spring back when gently pressed with the finger.

Meanwhile, preheat the oven to 400°F. Put the strudels in the oven, turn the heat down to 375°F and bake for 25 minutes or until a rich brown. Turn the strudels over for 5 minutes if necessary to brown the under side. Cool on a wire rack. Just before serving, sprinkle thickly with the confectioner's sugar.

Israeli Nusse Strudel

Makes: 4 strudels   **Freeze:** 3 months   **Keeps:** 1 week under refrigeration

Ingredients
Pastry
3 cups all-purpose flour plus 3 tsps baking powder
¾ cup plus 1 tbsp firm margarine or butter, cut in 1-inch chunks
⅔ cup soured cream

Filling
2 cups walnuts or pecans,
    coarsely chopped
½ cup raisins

½ cup white sugar
1 scant tbsp thin honey
2 tsps grated lemon rind

To spread on the dough
Apricot or another tart jam

Glaze
1 egg yolk mixed with 1 tsp cold water

To make the pastry, mix the flour with the chunks of fat and rub in or pulse until the particles of fat are the size of a filbert kernel. Tip into a bowl and mix to a dough with the soured cream. Divide into four, form each piece of dough into a little block about ½-inch thick, then wrap in foil and refrigerate overnight.

To make the filling, mix all the filling ingredients together to form a slightly tacky mixture, cover and leave.

Preheat the oven to 400°F and have ready two ungreased oven sheets. Roll out each portion of pastry in turn on a lightly floured board to make a rectangle about 11 inches by 6 inches. Spread the dough with a thin layer of jam, leaving ½ inch clear all the way round, then sprinkle it with a quarter of the filling. Turn in the ends and roll up, then lay, join side down, on the tray. Repeat with the remaining three pieces of dough and the rest of the nut filling.

Prick the strudels all over with a fork, brush them with the yolk and water mixture then bake for 10 minutes. Turn the heat down to 350°F and bake for a further 30-35 minutes or until the strudels are a rich brown. Carefully transfer to a cooling tray and allow to go cold. Cut the strudels into slices just before serving them, either plain or with a dusting of confectioners' sugar.

Cherry Strudel

Serves: 8 **Keeps:** 1 day under refrigeration

Ingredients

1 x 15oz can pitted sour red or
   black cherries
1½ cups dry cottage cheese or
   other medium-fat soft white cheese
¼ cup superfine sugar
1 egg yolk
Grated rind of ½ lemon
½ tsp vanilla extract

2 tbsps butter
¼-⅓ cup unsalted butter, melted
1 cup fresh breadcrumbs
¼ cup slivered almonds
6 sheets phyllo pastry, defrosted
1 tbsp granulated sugar mixed
   with 1 tbsp slivered almonds

Sauce

⅔ cup cherry syrup (from can)
2 tsps cornstarch mixed with
   1 tbsp each lemon juice
   and water

1 tbsp cherry brandy

Preheat the oven to 375°F. Have ready a lightly oiled cookie sheet.

Drain the cherries, reserving the syrup, and lay them on paper towels to absorb any moisture.

Mix together the cheese, sugar, egg yolk, lemon rind and vanilla. Melt the 2 tablespoons butter, add the crumbs and almonds and fry gently until golden-brown. Allow to cool.

Have ready 6 sheets of pastry, covered with a teatowel. Lay one sheet of pastry on a second teatowel, and with a pastry brush, paint the top surface very thinly with melted butter. Lay the next sheet on top, brush with butter, and repeat for each sheet in turn, stacking them one on top of the other until you have a pile of six. Leaving 2 inches of pastry bare on the edge nearest to you, spread the third of pastry nearest to you with half the buttered nut and crumb mixture. On top of this mixture lay the cheese filling in a strip about 2 inches wide. Lay the cherries on top of the cheese, and cover them in turn with the remaining crumbs.

Now lift up the teatowel and roll the bare pastry near you on to the filling, then turn in the sides and roll up the strudel. Place it, seam down, on the cookie sheet. Paint it all over with a little more melted butter and scatter with the slivered almonds mixed with the sugar. Bake for 35-40 minutes, or until golden-brown.

To make the cherry brandy sauce, put the cherry syrup into a small pan and bring to the boil. Stir in the cornstarch mixed with the lemon juice and water, bring to the boil again and bubble for 3 minutes or until the sauce looks clear. Stir in the cherry brandy. Serve warm or cold.

Streusel Kuchen
(Crumble Topped Cake)

Freeze: 6 months   **Keeps:** 3 days at room temperature

Ingredients
2 cups all-purpose flour
Pinch of salt
3 tsps baking powder
⅓ cup soft margarine
⅓ cup superfine sugar

1 egg
1 rounded tbsp apricot jam or
   ginger marmalade
⅔ cup milk

Streusel topping
½ cup all-purpose flour
2 tsps ground cinnamon

¾ cup brown sugar
¼ cup butter

Put all the cake ingredients into a bowl and beat by hand or machine until a thick, smooth batter is formed (2-3 minutes). Turn the batter into a greased pan 10 x 7 x 2 inches and level with a knife.

Make the streusel by mixing the flour, cinnamon and sugar. Melt the butter, then pour onto the dry ingredients and blend with a fork until evenly moistened and crumbly. Sprinkle the streusel evenly over the cake mixture.

Bake in a quick oven, 400°F, for 25-30 minutes or until golden brown.

The synagogue serves not only as a place of worship but also as a meeting place and as a place of study.

Gereybes
(Middle Eastern Shortbread)

Makes: about 30 biscuits **Freeze:** 1 month **Keeps:** 1 week in an airtight container

Ingredients
1 cup butter

⅔ cup superfine sugar

3 cups all-purpose flour

½ cup blanched almonds

Melt the butter gently then skim to remove the salt (or use saltless butter). Pour into a bowl and leave to set until creamy. Cream the butter and sugar until almost white then add the sifted flour a little at a time. Knead thoroughly. Leave to chill for 1 hour. Take pieces of the dough and roll each with the palm of the hand into a pencil shape about 7-inches long. Form into a bracelet (a little like a miniature bagel) and put an almond over the join. Arrange on ungreased trays, leaving 1 inch between each biscuit. Bake at 325°F for 20 minutes until a very pale gold and firm to the touch.

A Jewish scribe copying the Torah, the Jewish sacred writings which are used in synagogue services.

Apfelkuchen Squares

Makes: 24 squares   **Freeze:** 3 months   **Keeps:** 3 days under refrigeration

Ingredients

2 cups all-purpose flour
2 tsps baking powder
¾ cup soft margarine or butter
½ cup superfine sugar
Grated rind of ½ lemon
3 eggs

2lbs baking apples (weight when peeled and cored), thinly sliced
3 rounded tbsps granulated sugar
2 tbsps lemon juice
2 rounded tbsps apricot jam

Topping

¼ cup brown sugar

½ cup walnuts, finely chopped

Preheat the oven to 350°F. Grease a pan measuring approximately 12 x 8 x 1½ inches.

Put the flour, baking powder, fat, superfine sugar, lemon rind and eggs into a bowl and beat by hand, mixer or food processor until smooth. Take two-thirds of the mixture and spread it thinly over the base of the pan. Arrange the sliced applies in an even layer on top, sprinkle with the sugar and lemon juice and dot with the jam. Drop the remaining cake mixture by teaspoonfuls all over the apple filling and put in the oven.

After 10 minutes, open the oven, quickly smooth the blobs of cake mixture over the top of the apples with a large fork, then sprinkle evenly with the mixed nuts and sugar. Close the oven and bake for a further 30 minutes or until the cake is golden-brown and the apples feel tender when pierced with sharp knife.

Cut into 2-inch squares to serve.

Lekach
(Honey and Spice Cake)

Freeze: 1 month   **Keeps:** 1 week in an airtight container after cutting

Ingredients
2 cups all-purpose flour
¾ cup superfine sugar
1 tsp cinnamon
1 tsp mixed spice
¾ cup clear honey

½ cup cooking oil
2 eggs
1 tsp baking soda dissolved
     in 1½ cup orange juice
½ cup chopped walnuts

In a bowl, mix together the flour, sugar and spices. Make a well in center, then add the honey, oil and eggs. Beat well together until smooth. Dissolve the baking powder in the orange juice and add the nuts. Mix well with the cake batter. Pour into a wax paper lined pan approximately 10 x 8 x 2 inches. Bake at 325°F for 1¼ hours or until firm to the touch. When quite cold, wrap in foil. Keep for 1 week before cutting. Serve thinly sliced.

A menorah with nine lamps is used during the Hanukkah festival.

Sufganiyot
(Jelly-Filled Doughnuts)

Makes: 24   **Freeze:** 3 months   **Keeps:** 2 days under refrigeration

Ingredients
2 cakes fresh yeast
1¼ cups warm milk
1 tsp sugar
4 egg yolks
2 tbsps superfine sugar
4 cups all-purpose flour

Pinch of salt
½ cup very soft butter
Oil for deep-frying
Tart jam such as apricot or
    blackcurrant

Coating
Superfine sugar

Put the fresh yeast, ¼ cup of the warm milk and the 1 teaspoon sugar into a bowl, stir well, then leave to rise for 10 minutes. Put into the mixer bowl with all the remaining ingredients except the jam and the coating. Beat everything together for 5 minutes until the very soft dough looks smooth, shiny and elastic and will leave the sides of the bowl and the beater clean – this can be done with a wooden spoon or your hand, but it's hard work! Leave in the bowl, covered with saranwrap, and allow to rise until double in bulk – about 1½ hours.

Turn out onto a floured board and if the dough is at all sticky, work in a little more flour so that it is soft but easily rolled out. Roll out this dough ⅜-inch thick and cut into rounds about 2 inches across. Leave the rounds on the board, covered with a teatowel and let them rise until puffy, about 20 minutes.

Have ready a pan one-third full of oil, or a deep fryer, heated to 360° (when a cube of bread browns in 40 seconds). Fry the doughnuts in batches, leaving room for them to swell. They should be covered until the first side has browned – about 4 minutes – then uncover, turn them over and allow the second side to brown, then lift out and drain well on paper towels. Make a little slit in each doughnut and insert a teaspoon of the jam, then roll in the superfine sugar.